Sir David Attenborough
A Treasure Trove

SIR DAVID ATTENBOROUGH: A TREASURE TROVE

Copyright © Octopus Publishing Group Limited, 2025

All rights reserved.

No part of this book may be reproduced by any means, nor transmitted, nor translated into a machine language, without the written permission of the publishers.

Debbi Marco has asserted their right to be identified as the author of this work in accordance with sections 77 and 78 of the Copyright, Designs and Patents Act 1988.

Condition of Sale
This book is sold subject to the condition that it shall not, by way of trade or otherwise, be lent, resold, hired out or otherwise circulated in any form of binding or cover other than that in which it is published and without a similar condition including this condition being imposed on the subsequent purchaser.

An Hachette UK Company
www.hachette.co.uk

Summersdale Publishers
Part of Octopus Publishing Group Limited
Carmelite House
50 Victoria Embankment
LONDON
EC4Y 0DZ
UK

www.summersdale.com

This FSC® label means that materials used for the product have been responsibly sourced

The authorized representative in the EEA is Hachette Ireland, 8 Castlecourt Centre, Dublin 15, D15 XTP3, Ireland (email: info@hbgi.ie)

Printed and bound in Malaysia

ISBN: 978-1-83799-647-6

Substantial discounts on bulk quantities of Summersdale books are available to corporations, professional associations and other organizations. For details contact general enquiries: telephone: +44 (0) 1243 771107 or email: enquiries@summersdale.com.

SIR DAVID ATTENBOROUGH
A Treasure Trove

DEBBI MARCO

CONTENTS

Introduction	**6**
The Natural World	**8**
The Web of Life	**21**
The Animal Kingdom	**34**
Botanical Wonders	**46**
Our Blue Planet	**58**
Echoes of the Past	**69**
Guardians of the Earth	**80**
The Human Footprint	**91**
Hope for the Future	**102**
The Power of Nature	**113**
Answers	**124**

INTRODUCTION

The title "national treasure" is used a lot, and rarely is it so well deserved, but Sir David Attenborough (he was knighted in 1985) is most definitely one. Born in 1926, the broadcaster and biologist, who has graced our screens for decades, has dedicated his life to bringing the natural world to the attention of people who might otherwise have not taken too much notice of it. His dulcet tones and unscripted enthusiasm breathe life into the darkest depths of the oceans and the most remote regions of the Amazon and all that lies in between.

In his latter years, Attenborough's focus has been on climate change and activism. He has taken it upon himself to encourage people to not only respect and understand the planet we live on, but also consider how each one of our decisions and actions impacts all other living things – often to their detriment.

Within the pages of this book we celebrate all elements of David Attenborough's life and work, consider his most important messages, bring you his favourite facts about nature and his own life, and challenge you with trivia. So get ready to journey into the natural world with the most inspiring natural historian around.

The Natural World

I have been lucky enough to spend my life exploring the wild places of our planet and making films about the creatures that live there...
I have experienced the living world first-hand in all its variety and wonder, and witnessed some of its greatest spectacles and most gripping dramas.

FACT

David Attenborough grew up living on the campus of University College, Leicester, where his father, Frederick, was the principal. He loved collecting fossils and stones as a child, which inspired his love of the natural world. By the age of seven, David already had an impressive collection of birds' eggs and fossils, a passion that stayed with him through to adulthood.

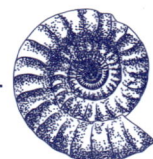

People depend on the natural world for sanity – in moments of crisis, the natural world is where they find solace. But it's also what feeds us and gives us the air that we breathe.

Each of us must cherish the natural world that surrounds us, from wide open countryside to tiny patches of green in our cities.

We have to recognize that every breath of air we take, every mouthful of food we take comes from the natural world. And that if we damage the natural world, we damage ourselves... We have the power. We have the knowledge to actually live in harmony with nature.

TRIVIA

David Attenborough has made and narrated many documentaries throughout his life, but what inspired Attenborough's programme *The Amber Time Machine*?

    a) His love of traffic lights

    b) A gift of amber containing prehistoric creatures from his adopted sister

    c) His interest in precious stones

David's long involvement with the BBC hasn't only been as a programme-maker; he has also held one of the most important positions at the organization. Which of these was it?

    a) Controller of BBC Two

    b) Main presenter of *BBC Nine O'Clock News*

    c) Director of Children and Education

People are discovering that they need the natural world for their very sanity. People who have never listened to a bird song are suddenly thrilled, excited, supported, inspired by the natural world. And they realize they're not apart from it. They are part of it.

I still recall, with great clarity, the very first time I went to the tropics... Wherever I looked, I found a prodigality of pattern and colour for which I was quite unprepared. It was a revelation of the splendour and fecundity of the natural world from which I have never recovered.

FACT

In 1945, David Attenborough won a scholarship to study at Cambridge University, where he was awarded a degree in natural sciences. Later, in the 1960s, he went on to study for a postgraduate degree in social anthropology at the London School of Economics. Over his lifetime, David has amassed 32 honorary degrees from universities around the world in recognition of his work.

One of the really great, profoundly moving experiences was to go to the giant sequoias in California, these enormous trees. It's not an accident that there's a cathedral-like feeling when you go amongst them. They are immense things, some of the tallest ones are enormous.

I'm very fond of South East Asia and especially Borneo. I've found it to be particularly rich in species of animals and plants that occur nowhere else.

The capture and distribution of the Sun's energy, and the cycling of carbon between the atmosphere and the living world that results, has been central to the activity of life on Earth for 3.5 billion years. In that time a host of forests, marshes, swamps, mats and blooms have brought power to the living world of their day.

FACT

One of David's favourite facts is that humans have spent hundreds of years documenting life on Earth. We now have a catalogue of around 1.6 million species, however, there may be 7 or 8 million more animal species that we don't yet know about. While David has dedicated his life to educating the public around different forms of nature and wildlife, it is humbling to think of how much is out there yet to be discovered.

In the Arctic, if it goes wrong, you're not just in mild trouble. Dropping a glove can mean losing your fingers.

The whole of life is coming to terms with yourself and the natural world. Why are you here? How do you fit in? What's it all about?

All organisms are ultimately concerned to pass on their genes to the next generation. That, it would seem to a dispassionate and clinical observer, is the prime objective of their existence. In the course of achieving it, they must face a whole succession of problems as they go through their lives. These problems are fundamentally the same whether the animals are spiders or squirrels, mice or monkeys, llamas or lobsters. The solutions developed by different species are hugely varied and often astounding. But they are all the more comprehensible and engaging for they are the trials we face ourselves.

The Web of Life

For life to truly thrive on this planet, there must be immense biodiversity. Only when billions of different individual organisms make the most of every resource and opportunity they encounter, and millions of species lead lives that interlock so that they sustain each other, can the planet run efficiently. The greater the biodiversity, the more secure will be all life on Earth, including ourselves.

FACT

Most people know all about the circle of life and the food chain where many animals thrive because they eat others. But David highlights the interconnectivity of all species, including how humans are connected to and reliant on different animals in the most curious of ways. One of his favourite facts is that there is a fungus which grows on the fur of sloths that could treat some types of cancer, highlighting how we all live in an interconnected web with nature.

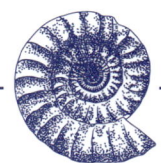

Since termites are among the few creatures able to convert rotting vegetation into living tissue, they are a crucial link in the flow of nutrients from one organism to another. Many creatures feed on them. Some kinds of ants exist almost entirely by raiding termite nests and carrying off the grubs and workers for food. Birds and frogs sit beside the marching columns wherever they are exposed, picking off individuals one at a time while the rest of the column marches doggedly onwards.

It is amazing how much the natural world can come into our cities. Most of our cities, thank goodness, have parks of one kind or another... you would be astonished at how much stuff you can see there. How many different butterflies, how many different kinds of birds.

Few big animals are truly solitary independent individuals. A buffalo standing in a swamp stolidly chewing the cud is not alone. Oxpeckers cling to its flanks. Ticks are boring into its hide. Leeches may have fastened on to it when it went to drink and now lie within its mouth attached to its lips. Tapeworms hidden from view, may be trailing through its convoluted gut, roundworms encysted in its muscles and flukes moored in the veins of its liver absorbing its blood. All these creatures are robbing it of sustenance. But there are still others, even smaller, which are providing it with food and without these it would starve.

FACT

It's a common misconception that wildlife and plant species are found in all corners of the Earth, when actually the concentration of the different species is huge. It is thought that 70 per cent of the world's species are found in just 12 countries: Ecuador, India, Indonesia, Madagascar, Australia, Brazil, the Democratic Republic of the Congo, Mexico, China, Colombia, Costa Rica and Peru. Rainforests are thought to contain up to 90 per cent of all species; they are also home to 30 per cent of the total bird species, while two-thirds of 250,000 known plant species can be found in tropical regions.

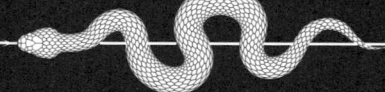

How do you persuade people that the wildlife around us is under such pressure? The first thing is that you show people things… and suddenly they become aware that these things that they've only seen in picture books or on television are real things and living there, but the locals have got to realize that they are valuable… that people will come from different continents simply to see the splendours that you have.

One species of insect may live on just one species of plant, perched on one species of tree. The result is a baffling complexity of interconnected relationships – every species a critical component of the whole.

FACT

As is fitting for a naturalist of his profile, David has more than 40 plants and animals named after him including the Attenborough hawkweed – a member of the daisy family. A Madagascan dragonfly was even named after David as a present for his ninetieth birthday. The UK's new polar research vessel, RRS *Sir David Attenborough* also bears his name.

Only two major environments have apparently remained physically unchanged over vast periods of time – the jungle and the sea. Even here, [in the Himalayas] the landmasses bearing the tropical jungles have changed as the continents have moved.

It is no accident that the planet's stability has wavered just as its biodiversity has declined – the two things are bound together. To restore stability to our planet, therefore, we must restore its biodiversity, the very thing we have removed.

We must recapture billions of tons of carbon from the air, and fix our sights on keeping one and a half degrees within reach. A new industrial revolution, powered by millions of sustainable innovations, is essential, and is indeed already beginning.

TRIVIA

As part of his travels, David has been lucky enough to experience many different cultures and has eaten lots of unusual animals. But what does David claim to be the most exotic thing he's ever eaten?

a) Snakes
b) Moth caterpillars
c) Crickets

David has visited most countries in the world to make his documentaries. But which has he described as his favourite country?

a) Scotland
b) China
c) Australia

FACT

Much research has been done into how fossils were formed. It is universally agreed that the first forests grew around 300 million years ago in tropical freshwater swamps. As the trees died, they fell into the swamps and became entombed in sediment. Over millions of years, more and more layers of sediment built up and were compressed, gradually turning into rock. Meanwhile, water would seep into the rock. Minerals in the water eventually replaced the wood. And all that is left is a stone copy, or a fossil.

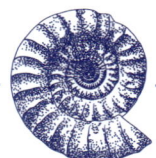

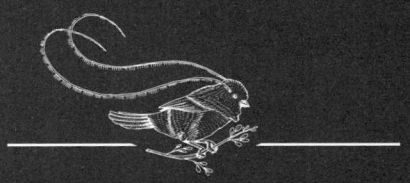

Darwin revealed that all species have evolved over time to best exploit the conditions in which they live. He further realized that these conditions are not simply those of geography and climate, but also their relationship to other lives that live alongside. From the delicate co-dependencies of bees and orchids to the dramatic connection between cheetah and gazelle, all life on Earth is both product and contributor to its place in space and time. This complex web of life of which we are a part has been millennia in the making.

The Animal Kingdom

[Animals] have a number of qualities that are unique to them. They're not trying to sell you anything and they're not telling you lies. They are unpredictable. They are very often new. They're extraordinarily beautiful. They're dramatic. And they share something with us, which is life.

FACT

David's career in the study of animals started from an early age. When he was a young boy, David sold newts to the zoology department at his father's university. He never told them, but the newts were sourced from the pond right next to the department building and he was merely scooping them out.

A picture of a gorilla with its baby moves the hearts of every single human being on this planet... and we can explain how we depend upon them, how we are part of them. And when we are saving them, we are saving ourselves.

I was about to start [talking to the camera] when there was a great weight on my head. And I turned round and there was an enormous female gorilla. While she was doing that, I suddenly felt two baby gorillas undoing my shoelaces. I wasn't in the least frightened. They were totally friendly. It was interesting really because you empathized – you knew perfectly well that they were not aggressive.

Unjustifiable anthropomorphism is the danger. You have to be very careful when you're writing it that every time you say an animal "is jealous", you are absolutely sure there is scientific evidence to make sure what you're saying is correct.

I would come back as a sloth. Hanging from a tree, chewing leaves sounds great.

I have been in a Land Rover that was charged by a rhinoceros, and that was tiresome. But if you are making natural history films, what you are trying to do is show the animal as it normally lives, and animals don't normally spend their time attacking human beings.

TRIVIA

One of David's first presenting jobs was on a children's TV programme in 1975 about mythical creatures. What was it called?

a) *Fabulous Animals*

b) *U is for Unicorn*

c) *Fantasy Animals*

David has been given honorary degrees for his work by a huge number of British universities, but how many?

a) 16

b) 25

c) 32

The king cobra is getting on for ten feet long... and it can rear up... it makes a sort of growling noise when it does.

We were the first people, I think, to film... birds of paradise in display in the wild... and they are unforgettably beautiful.

There are lots of things that live perfectly well in captivity and you can give them all they need. Equally there are things that should not, under any circumstances, be kept in captivity. You should not keep raptors, you shouldn't keep eagles in captivity. Dreadful. I don't think that you should keep lions in captivity, unless you can provide them with an enormous area. I wouldn't myself keep gorillas. I mean, that's a very difficult thing. They are highly intelligent animals. I suppose there are possibilities, but I wouldn't risk it.

FACT

Very few people do not recognize David Attenborough's soothing tones. But did you know David narrated every episode (over 250 of them) of *Wildlife on One*, a BBC series that ran between 1977 and 2005. The episode on meerkats, broadcast in 1987, was voted the best wildlife documentary of all time by BBC viewers.

Sometimes a problem is more complicated than it seems. I watched something which was absolutely agonizing – a small baby elephant that was dying of thirst and the whole family was several days from water. This poor little thing was dying and you think, why didn't you give it a bucket of water? But you're in the desert and you don't have a bucket of water and the thing is very close to death and has to walk for another three days if it was going to get to water, so all you're doing is prolonging the death. All you can do there is watch tragedy. But tragedy is part of life and you have to show it. You can't have sunshine throughout your life. To have done anything else would only have made matters worse and distort the truth.

You don't get tired of animals but you
can get tired of people quite easily.

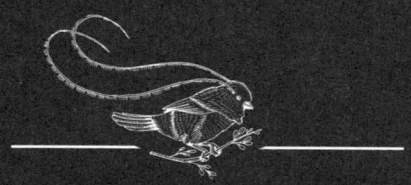

What do you do about conserving an animal that eats people? In the Sundarbans in India, tigers still eat a person every month. It's all very well for us in the West saying, "It's wonderful, it's poetry", but then my son has not been eaten by a tiger. If he had been, I would take a different view of tigers, especially if they were roaming in Richmond Park. If one was coming into my garden and knocking off my babies, I would feel differently about it. I would be saying to the people in New York who are banging on saying, "You've got to protect the tigers", "Come over here, mate. It's a tough, tough problem."

TRIVIA

David Attenborough doesn't count himself as a lover of any particular animal as he is interested in them all, but there is one animal he can't stand. Is it…

a) Dogs

b) Spiders

c) Rats

At 11 years old, David's first "job" was selling one type of animal he found to the zoology department of University College, Leicester, for three pence each. Were they…

a) Mice

b) Butterflies

c) Newts

Botanical Wonders

The world has suddenly become plant-conscious. There's an awareness that we would starve without plants, we wouldn't be able to breathe without plants. And yet people's understanding about plants, except in a very kind of narrow way, has not kept up with that. I think this [documentary] will bring it home.

FACT

Kelp is the fastest-growing seaweed on Earth. It is able to increase the length of its broad brown fronds by as much as half a metre in a single day. Kelp is home to around 800 creatures and is harvested in a way very similar to wheat. It's used for many things; most notably a substance called algin is extracted to be used in lipstick, ice cream and toothpaste. Kelp is also used as a natural dye for clothes.

We know what a greenhouse is like... everything grows very fast, and that's what the jungle is like. So we've got this tremendous proliferation of life.

Until you've actually seen in 3D a flower opening, you can't imagine how wonderful, transcendental and hypnotic, thrilling and enlightening the whole thing is. It's just stunning.

FACT

In 1803, a packet of seeds was found in a captured ship and the seeds were stored in the Tower of London. The seeds were collected by Jan Teerlink, a Dutch merchant, who was on board the ship. Jan had collected 38 different types of seed. The perfectly preserved seeds were discovered and sent to Kew Royal Botanic Gardens 200 years later. Experts managed to germinate three of the seeds and a pincushion plant was grown from one, showing us how robust seeds can be.

Forests are very vulnerable, very tempting for people who want to make a quick buck. Because they are easy money. You cut the forest down and you sell the timber and having done that, the land that has been cleared you can plant soy, you can plant palm oil which we in the West use in such great quantities. So we are responsible because of what we buy for the quick profit people can get from their forests. And it's crucially important to remember they are even more valuable than that because they are the most critical element in a whole complex of climate and rainfall and fertility that keeps the natural world going. They're precious and they become more and more precious as in fact more and more of them are being cut down.

TRIVIA

Sir David Attenborough is vocal about his love of trees. He even has a favourite tree that he visits and checks on regularly especially after a storm. What is it?

    a) A Canadian redwood in Kew Gardens

    b) An ancient oak in Richmond Park

    c) A weeping willow by the River Thames

Which of the following has David never done?

    a) Driven a car

    b) Sent an email

    c) Been in a submarine

Over half the population of the world, according to the United Nations, is urbanized, lives in cities, only sees cultivated plants and never sees a wild community of plants. But that wild community is there and we depend upon it. And we better jolly well care for it.

The great forests are far more varied than their uniform smooth trunks and nearly identical spear-shaped leaves suggest. Only when they produce their flowers is it evident how many species there are among them. The numbers are astounding. In one hectare of jungle, it is common to find well over a hundred different kinds of tall tree.

What we don't realize is that plants are not passive, they move, and they communicate.

I've had a pitcher plant named after me – Nepenthes attenboroughii – and I have one of the few plants in captivity. It's in my front room and I say good morning to it every day and ask how it's getting on, would it like a fly or something, because they're carnivorous.

FACT

The beautiful giant waterlily is actually a vicious, murderous bully that crushes, spears and blocks light from all its competitors ensuring it survives above all other plant species. It's one of the most aggressive empire-building plants there is. The world's largest waterlily, discovered in North Bolivia, is bigger than a double bed.

I really wanted to see a jungle... I thought there would be monkeys hanging from every tree and snakes wherever you put your foot, but it isn't like that at all of course... Europe's fine but it's not as rich as the jungle and that's very exciting.

Plants fight and strangle one another... You can see a plant suddenly putting out a tentacle. You know it can't actually see, but you can watch it trying to find its victim. Then, when it does, it wraps around the victim quickly and strangles it. It's tough stuff.

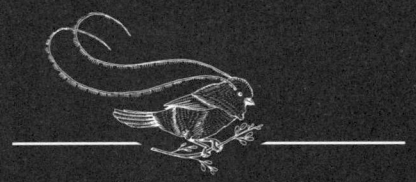

The Amazon is tens of millions of years old. In that time, it has covered roughly the same patch of Earth with its vast closed canopy as it did until recently, thriving in one of the planet's prime pitches. The amount of sunlight and rainfall it has received and the level of nutrients in its soil may have been roughly constant throughout… it is the most biodiverse place on the planet – the most successful of life's current enterprises.

Our Blue Planet

Why are coral reefs so beautiful and colourful? It is not immediately obvious, though the wildlife is wonderful: shell-less molluscs, crustaceans and shoals of fish that do not give a damn whether you are there or not. Your first trip to a coral reef will be one of the most transforming moments of your life.

FACT

Anglerfish are one of the most unusual fish in that they act like "fishermen" to capture their prey. Instead of a rod and line like their human counterparts, anglerfish dangle their long dorsal spine in front of their mouths. This has a tiny membrane which the fish shake just like a fisherman's lure, but this only works for shallow-sea anglerfish. A deep-sea anglerfish's dorsal spine has a lure at the end of the rod. This has bioluminescent bacterial light that attracts its prey. Small fish are attracted to the lure, swimming closer to the anglerfish until they are near enough to be sucked into its mouth.

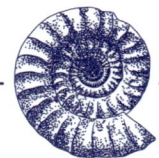

Visiting a coral reef is a fundamentally different wildlife encounter from anything I have known on land.

The filming of killer whales tipping ice floes and knocking seals off was an unbelievable achievement.

FACT

Some fish can swim faster than a cheetah – the fastest land animal – can run. Most notably the black marlin has been recorded swimming at 129 kilometres an hour, while the sailfish has been clocked swimming at 110 kilometres an hour.

TRIVIA

The *Blue Planet* series captivated audiences across the globe, but the award-winning series wasn't easy or quick to film. How many years did it take to make David Attenborough's award-winning television series *Blue Planet II*?

    a) Four years

    b) One year

    c) Ten years

David isn't the only talented member of his family. His brother Richard was an actor and film director. Richard won the Oscar for best director for which film?

    a) *Cry Freedom*

    b) *Gandhi*

    c) *Oh! What a Lovely War*

The ocean's power of regeneration is remarkable – if we just offer it the chance. We are in reach of a whole new relationship with the ocean, a wiser, more sustainable relationship. The choice lies with us.

The world is much more complex and much more sentient than one supposes. Fish are much cleverer than we thought. They have more personalities than we think.

Most of our planet is covered by water. There is so much of it that if all the mountains of the world were levelled and their debris dumped into the oceans, then the surface of the globe would be entirely submerged beneath water to a depth of several thousand metres.

FACT

David loves to marvel at different fish but one that he finds most interesting is tuna: there are 30 different species of tuna including albacore, skipjack and king mackerel. Some of them grow as big as four metres and are as heavy as 650 kilos. They often swim in large groups, known as schools, that are up to 19 miles wide.

# TRIVIA

In 2016 and 2017 a significant number of corals in the Great Barrier Reef died as a result of the warming of the seas. How many was it?

    a) 100 per cent

    b) 30 per cent

    c) 50 per cent

David's first television hit was the series *Life on Earth* in 1979. How many people around the world are estimated to have watched it?

    a) 10 million

    b) 120 million

    c) 500 million

People say, "What was the most magical moment in your career as a naturalist?" and I always reply, "The first time I put on a mask and went below the surface and moved in three dimensions with just the flick of a fin, and suddenly saw all these amazing multi-coloured things living in communities right there... You're not harnessed by gravity anymore. You're free. It's bliss. An extraordinary experience, like going into space. There's no equivalent anywhere else in the natural world of such splendour: all of these things moving through an architecture of coral."

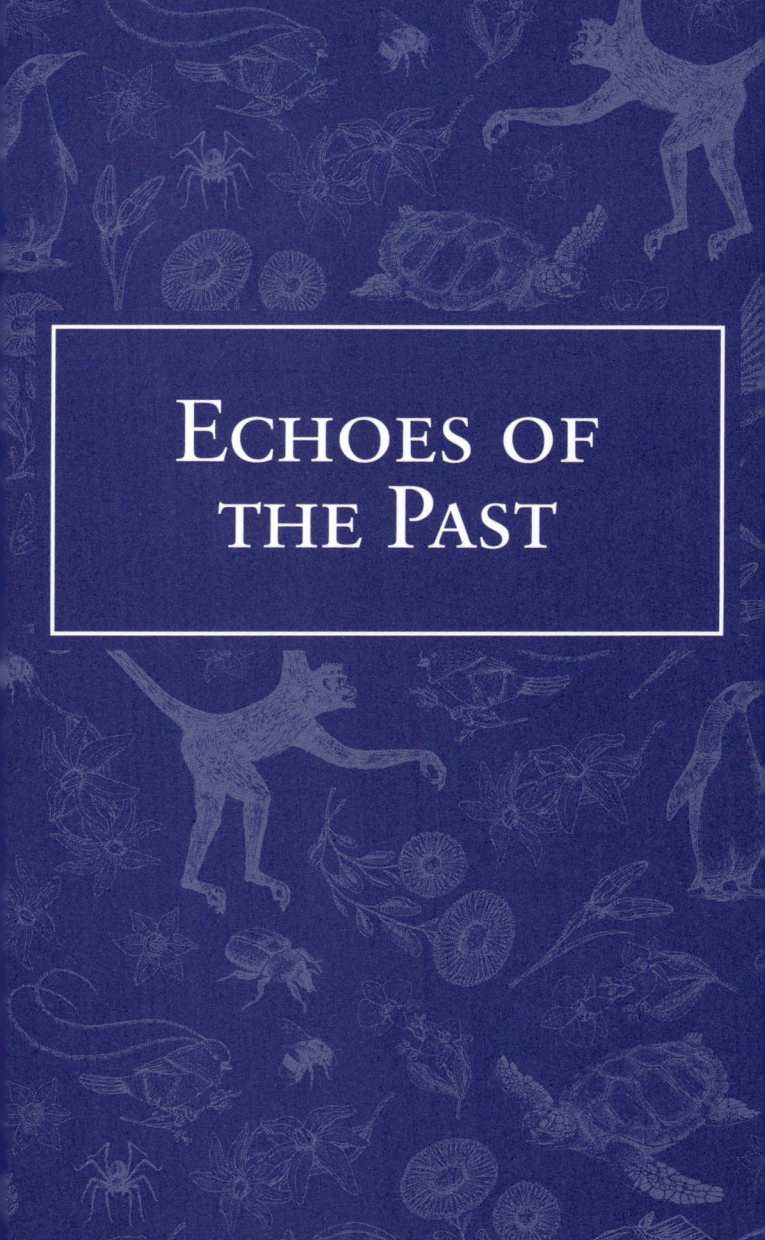

Echoes of the Past

An object the size of Mount Everest hit the Earth and that was the end of the Cretaceous — and that's an extraordinary thing to happen. And of course it's extraordinary too because it caused the end of the dinosaurs. And the life on this planet, had to restart.

FACT

One of the first dinosaurs to be discovered and named was an iguana-like beast subsequently named iguanodon. Only a collection of its teeth were found in 1822 by Mary Ann Mantell in Sussex, on the south coast of England. The teeth, embedded in rock, indicated this giant lizard measured around ten metres in length.

Crocodiles existed throughout the period of the dinosaurs, and the reason they weren't exterminated is because they lived in water – and the ecosystems in fresh water recovered probably earlier than many on the land.

The skull is the most important part of an animal, and what you can deduce from the skull is absolutely fascinating. Imagine that you were from Mars, and when you landed on Earth all you could find were human skeletons but not a single one with a skull. You wouldn't know anything about it at all – you wouldn't know what it fed on, how it could move, you wouldn't know what it could see – it would be useless.

There have been enormous discoveries about fossils in China over the past 20 or 30 years, and the most dramatic was that they found dinosaurs with feathers. That answers some of the questions about the evolution of birds.

When you first see one of these things, in the bones, and certainly in the reconstructions, it takes your breath away, but you really then want to start asking questions. Very simple questions like, how did they mate? How did they catch their food? How fast can they run? Were they aggressive?

I would love to see a pterosaur. They were the size of small aeroplanes.

TRIVIA

As a giant in the world of naturalists, it's unsurprising that David Attenborough has more than 40 creatures and plants named after him, including a dinosaur. What is it called?

      a) Davidosaurus

      b) D'ythinkhesaurus

      c) Attenborosaurus

Another creature named after David is a lizard named *Platysaurus attenboroughi*. But what is its common name?

      a) Fat lizard

      b) Flat lizard

      c) Sprat lizard

FACT

Of all the creatures, David would most like to bring the quetzalcoatlus, the largest pterosaur and largest flying creature, back from extinction. He says his reason is that although dinosaur experts make programmes about it, they still don't know one of the most basic facts about it: how it took off for flight.

I don't think an interest in the natural world needs to be confined to the creatures of the living. I first became really intoxicated with the natural world as a boy collecting fossils in the middle of England. They were shell fossils, but they were nonetheless very romantic.

FACT

In an interview, David Attenborough once asked expert Dr Andre Rowe who would win in a fight between a Tyrannosaurus rex and a giant pliosaur, which was recently found on the south coast of England. The pliosaur was the subject of David's documentary *Attenborough and the Giant Sea Monster*. It was quite a schoolboy question but the palaeontologist obliged with an answer: the winner would be the pliosaur.

The really nice thing is that we can use technology like never before. We can laser-scan bones to make replicas within a millimetre's accuracy and we use CT scanners. We can do so much more than we could 20 years ago, even on the same bones.

I've got dinosaur footprints... Dinosaur footprints are quite common in Texas. You can buy 100 yards of dinosaur footprints.

TRIVIA

David once met a tortoise on the Galapagos Islands, which was thought to be extinct and was the last of its kind. What was it called?

a) Lonesome George

b) Billy no-mates

c) Lonely Louis

Which of the following shows do not owe their existence to David?

a) *Dad's Army*

b) *Monty Python's Flying Circus*

c) *Pot Black*

Guardians of the Earth

It has never happened in the entire history of mankind that neighbours have agreed for a long time, let alone the whole world, but the longer we delay climate laws, the greater the penalties will be. The longer we delay, the longer the droughts, disasters and famine. The more people will die until the world comes to its senses. It won't be easy.

FACT

Attenborough was initially sceptical about the impact of humans on climate change but was finally convinced by a lecture he attended in 2004; however, he didn't speak publicly on the issue until two years later. Since then he has been a passionate environmental activist, even addressing COP26 in 2021, and asking world leaders to take steps to reduce emissions.

Nature is far from unlimited. The wild is finite. It needs protecting.

People are listening... There was a time 30 years ago when it really looked as though we might certainly exterminate several species of big whales; fishing nations, maritime nations of the world did get together and say, "Okay, unless we do something we're going to lose everything."

We have got to control the human population, we really have. Everything you can think of, whether it is violence in the cities, or wars, or poisoning the ocean, it's all due to population. It's the underlying cause. There is no problem facing the world today that wouldn't be easier if there were fewer people. Not one. And we don't talk about it.

What we're going to do about 1.5 degrees rise in the temperature of the ocean over the next ten years, I don't know, but we could actually do something about plastic right now.

The Holocene has ended. The Garden of Eden is no more. We have changed the world so much that scientists say we are in a new geological age. We need to move beyond guilt or blame and get on with the practical tasks at hand.

TRIVIA

As a keen campaigner around climate change, what is the one thing David urges everyone to think about and change their habits around in order to save the planet?

> a) Eating too much meat
>
> b) Driving petrol cars
>
> c) Wasting resources

David is famous for introducing audiences to new creatures. On his first ever nature show, *Zoo Quest*, which beast was captured on film for the first time?

> a) Scarlet macaw
>
> b) Komodo dragon
>
> c) Pygmy octopus

It is difficult to overstate it. We are now so numerous, so powerful, so all-pervasive, the mechanisms that we have for destruction are so wholesale and so frightening, that we can actually exterminate whole ecosystems without even noticing it.

The scientific evidence is that if we have not taken dramatic action in the next decade, we could face irreversible damage to the natural world and the collapse of our societies.

Knowledge can't have a cash value. Facts don't have cash values. It's just part of life. To know your imagination of the different worlds that once existed, it's enriching and makes you more appreciative of the fact that you're alive. The evidence goes back for all these millions of years and that's part of the meaning of life really.

FACT

David is keen to highlight how positive action can help to reverse the damage that mankind has inflicted on the world. One example he cites is in Costa Rica, where the government offered grants to landowners to replace the trees that had been logged. The loss of trees in 100 years, between 1880 and 1980, was staggering with only one quarter of the country still covered by forests compared to three quarters a century earlier. But, David happily reports, this loss has been reversed since the grants were offered and the forest has returned to cover half of Costa Rica.

For a long time it suited people to bury their heads in the sand, but it is to do with us, and we know about the way the world works. That's what science is about.

Self-interest is for the past; common interest is for the future.

We all need a healthy ocean, so we must change our ways. Together with the right management, we can repopulate the seas. We can reduce marine pollution and minimize the impact of ocean acidification. The ocean's power of regeneration is remarkable if we just offer it the chance. It's not too late.

The Human Footprint

Stop waste. Stop waste of any kind. Stop wasting power, stop wasting food, stop wasting plastic. Don't waste, this is a precious world. Celebrate and cherish.

FACT

As part of his desire to protect the planet, David Attenborough is very careful around what he eats. While he doesn't describe himself as a vegetarian, and still eats fish and cheese, he has become more vegetarian over the past few years than he imagined he would be.

You have got an albatross that comes back to feed its young. In close-up, it regurgitates the stuff it has been collecting round the world's oceans for ten days to feed its chicks and what comes out? Bits of plastic. And then you see the chicks swallowing this plastic. If you warm the plastic, it gives off dioxins.

The world is not a bowl of fruit from which we can just take what we wish. We are part of it and if we destroy it we destroy ourselves.

The question is, are we going to be in time, and are we going to do enough? And the answer to both of those is no. We won't be able to do enough to mend everything. But we can make it a darn sight better than it would be if we didn't do anything at all.

I would say that the time has come to put aside national ambitions and look for an international ambition of survival.

I belong to the generation that really created all this stuff. We had no concept that we were ruining the world, none. I suppose you can say, well, you were very insensitive, you should have realized, but I don't think many people did.

TRIVIA

In 2019, which country dropped GDP as a primary measure of economic success, instead focusing on its most pressing national concerns: people and planet?

a) China

b) United States

c) New Zealand

David's encounter with gorillas in Rwanda is one of the most famous pieces of television in history. But what item did the baby gorillas try to steal from him?

a) Microphone

b) Trousers

c) Shoes

We have time now – perhaps ten years, perhaps 20 years to do something about it, but the longer we leave it, the more difficult it will be.

One of the most magical moments of a naturalist's life is the first time you dive on a coral reef. We were filming Blue Planet *and we got there expecting to see the most beautiful spectacle imaginable. We dived down and it was gone. Dead. Because of humans. I just felt… horror.*

The big demand that we've imposed on the planet is to get meat. That's what's taken over so much of our countryside. That's what's causing the Brazilian rainforest to be knocked down, to turn it into grazing – for more hamburgers. We can't afford to do that anymore and sustain the number of people we've got.

FACT

The Amazon rainforest is at risk of something called "dieback" – this is when a rainforest is unable to produce enough moisture to feed the rainclouds it relies on to "self-feed". Sadly the Amazon is predicted to be reduced to 75 per cent of its original size by the 2030s. This gloomy prediction means in just over five years, the Amazon could begin to die out and thousands of animals and plant species will die out along with it.

Fifty years ago, I used to go along, chase a giant anteater and pull it by the tail so we could film it. I am sorry about that sort of thing. But those were different days.

Puffins are dependent on sand eels for feeding their chicks but the sand eel population, because of the warming water, has moved away. What the puffins have been taking to is pipefish, which are hard, spiky fish which are making the chicks choke.

Man has as it were a biological right to exist just like everything else. I'm not suggesting that... man should exterminate himself, God forbid. Neither am I suggesting that he shouldn't actually grow crops, of course he must. What I'm suggesting is that he shouldn't put everything else in jeopardy in order to do so.

Hope for the Future

The truth is, every one of us, no matter who we are or where we live, can and must play a part in restoring nature. It's easy to feel overwhelmed or powerless by the scale of the issues facing our planet, but we have the solutions. I am hopeful for the future, because although nature is in crisis, now is the time for action, and together we can save it.

FACT

One thing that David Attenborough tries hard to hold on to is hope, and he looks for glimpses of it in every corner of the planet. Despite the gloomy predictions of climate change and erosion of ice blocks, he was thrilled that in 2020, for the first time in 600 years, white stork chicks hatched – with a little help from some conservation experts in the south of England.

If I have to grasp for little threads of hope, one is that humans are going to be better informed about the state of the world than they have ever been in the planet's history. Kids in Tibet are going to be talking to people in Patagonia about what is happening to the Earth and there is a chance that a worldwide, slow protest movement will grow with younger people wanting something to be done.

There's a huge movement around the world of people from all nations, young people who can see what is happening to the world, and demanding that their government should take action. And that's – that's the best hope that I have. I mean, it's – obviously my generation failed. We've allowed it to happen.

We have to recognize that the Earth and its oceans are finite. We have to recognize that in the past we have destroyed whole fisheries, herring, cod, just destroyed them... We need to show restraint. Mutual restraint. We have to know we aren't always in competition with one another.

There is now a bigger sympathy for the natural world among city-dwellers than there ever was. Our comprehension of the animal kingdom has changed beyond recognition.

The world belongs to the younger people. I have had my go. The younger generation is very, very passionate and concerned about the next 60 or 70 years facing them.

TRIVIA

What is one of the things David recommends you can do to bring wildlife into your garden?

      a) Plant wildflowers

      b) Create a pond

      c) Leave food out

During filming for the BBC's 2002 *Life of Mammals* documentary series, David brilliantly impersonated the call of a creature in order to bring it closer to the camera. Which?

      a) Wolf

      b) Elephant

      c) Barn owl

*I am an ardent recycler. I would like to
think that it works. I don't know whether
it does or not. I put in all these bulbs that
mean I can't see anything for more than
30 seconds. I don't put an electric fire on if
I don't need it. I do put on a sweater. I am
installing solar panels in my house at the
moment. It is all a tremendous fiddle and
you just hope it is going to contribute.*

*The natural world doesn't belong entirely to us.
We have a moral responsibility to the natural
world as well as a practical one not to screw it
up, otherwise we are going to be in big trouble.*

We have a responsibility, every one of us. We may think we live a long way from the ocean, but we don't. What we actually do here, and in the middle of Asia or wherever, has a direct effect on the ocean and what the oceans do reflect back on us. It is one world, and for the first time in the history of mankind, for the first time in 500 million years, one species has the future in the palm of its hands. I just hope it realizes that is the case.

FACT

David often cites the importance of working together to create meaningful change. In the 1940s it was clear some whales were going to become extinct. It took 40 years for nations to come together to decide to act. But when the International Whaling Commission banned whaling in 1982, the results were spectacular, and the whales are back in the ocean including very rare species which are now present in big numbers.

*The truth is: the natural world is
changing. And we are totally dependent
on that world. It provides our food, water
and air. It is the most precious thing
we have and we need to defend it.*

*There has been a worldwide shift,
I think, amongst people in general about
the concern there should be for the
natural world. I am encouraged more
than I have been for some time.*

We now stand at a unique point in our planet's history, one where we must all share responsibility both for our present well-being and for the future of life on Earth.

The Power of Nature

The natural world is wonderful enough. You don't have to distort anything. What's out there is so beautiful, so absorbing and so stunning, if you present it honestly there's no need to over-sentimentalize it, no need to make it more awesome than it is. Let it speak for itself. This world is good enough for me thanks.

FACT

There's no arguing that David Attenborough is well travelled but he takes his work seriously and commits to each television series he makes. In fact, in order to make just one series of *Life on Earth* the intrepid naturalist travelled 1.5 million miles and visited over 30 countries in order to film more than 600 species of animals and plants.

*In my time I could, and did, get on a bicycle
and cycle 15 miles to a quarry and spend
the day looking for dragonflies, grass
snakes and newts, as well as fossils.*

Animal behaviour is perhaps the most obviously
exciting aspect of natural history. It is full of action
and drama – a killer whale surging up a beach to
grab a young sea-lion; an ant navigating across a
Saharan sand dune by taking repeated observations
of the sun; a mother bat fighting through crowds
of begging infants on the roof of a cave in order
to give her milk to her own baby and no other.

We all know in our heart of hearts how important the natural world is. It's okay for me, I've got a garden. I think of those people who don't. That deprivation. But if you've got a garden, and you've been forced to sit in it for some time because of Covid, you know how important it is.

I've been fantastically lucky, I suppose. I've been everywhere I've ever wanted to be. The riches I've seen. The pleasures that I've had. These things are overwhelming.

Birdwatchers are a particular breed, whereas I'm as interested in caterpillars, sticklebacks and dragonflies as birds.

TRIVIA

Unsurprisingly, David's love of nature was nurtured from a young age and his first pet, given to him by his dad at the age of eight, also helped to inspire his love of nature. But what did his dad give him?

>   a) A puppy
>   b) A goldfish
>   c) A fire salamander

Still out in nature at the age of 95, David suffered a badly injured hand despite wearing thick gloves after an encounter with a...?

>   a) Shark
>   b) Cactus
>   c) Camera tripod

FACT

Dragonflies were the first insects ever to fly 300 million years ago, long before birds. While modern dragonflies have small wings, just two to five inches in span, fossilized dragonflies boast wingspans of up to 24 inches. No wonder these amazing creatures are one of David's favourites!

I remember getting up before dawn and going to a hide we had built by a billabong in northern Australia. Going there in the pitch dark and just watching dawn, watching the animals coming to this billabong in front of you, seeing the birds arrive and the kangaroos coming out and then seeing the crocs gliding across the top, and pythons snaking through the water and then these wonderful ibis and magpie geese and the sun coming up and the whole thing, I mean you suddenly saw a kind of prelapsarian, paradisiacal, Rousseauesque, Brueghel-like world of the Garden of Eden.

FACT

David does his best to support as many organizations as possible who work for the good of the natural world. He is a patron of the British Dragonfly Society, president of Butterfly Conservation and a member of the RSPB. He has also been awarded the Rothschild medal in recognition of his services to The Wildlife Trusts.

TRIVIA

As well as fossils, David used to collect exotic pets – although he's said that in hindsight he possibly shouldn't have done so in many cases. But what did David used to keep as a pet in his garden?

      a) A three-legged hedgehog

      b) A chicken

      c) An earthworm

David's first boss at the BBC thought he should not appear on camera because his what was too big?

      a) His head

      b) His teeth

      c) His ego

Experience has taught me how amazingly big and unpredictable the natural world is. When you're young, you think you know it all about the natural world... But in fact we only know a tiny proportion about the complexity of the natural world. Wherever you look, there are still things we don't know about and don't understand, as recent discoveries about, say, the behaviours of pufferfish and peacock spiders prove. There are always new things to find out if you go looking for them. They will last me out!

ANSWERS

Page 13: **b, a**

Page 31: **b, c**

Page 39: **a, c**

Page 45: **c, c**

Page 52: **b, a**

Page 63: **a, b**

Page 67: **c, c**

Page 74: **c, b**

Page 79: **a, a**

Page 85: **c, b**

Page 96: **c, c**

Page 107: **b, a**

Page 118: **c, b**

Page 122: **a, b**

Jane Austen: A Treasure Trove

Constance Moore

Hardback

ISBN: 978-1-83799-645-2

Throughout the ages, Jane Austen has charmed and delighted readers with her sharp wit and insightful commentary on society's foibles. This exquisite collection of classic quotations, fascinating facts and trivia questions captures the essence of her timeless wisdom, making it a must-have for both new readers and seasoned enthusiasts. Each page is filled with tart humour, astute observations, and the essential truths of love and life, showcasing Austen at her finest.

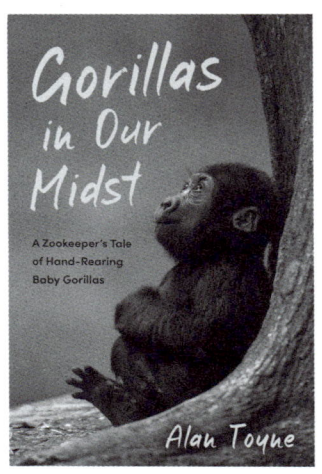

Gorillas in Our Midst: A Zookeeper's Tale of Hand-Rearing Baby Gorillas

Alan Toyne

Paperback

ISBN: 978-1-83799-525-7

When Afia, a newborn Western Lowland Gorilla, is rejected by her mother Kera, her human keeper Alan must start the challenging – but rewarding – experience of hand-rearing her at home. *Gorillas in Our Midst* offers a unique glimpse into the intricate world of primate social dynamics, in all their complicated, human-like glory.

IMAGE CREDITS

Cover and pp.5, 8, 13, 21, 34, 39, 46, 52, 58, 67, 69, 79, 80, 91, 96, 102, 113, 118, 124 – spider © alyaBigJoy/Shutterstock.com; cover and pp.7, 8, 9, 21, 22, 34, 35, 46, 58, 59, 69, 70, 80, 90, 91, 101, 102, 113 – penguins © Arthur Balitskii/Shutterstock.com; cover and pp.8, 11, 16, 21, 24, 29, 34, 40, 46, 49, 54, 58, 61, 69, 72, 80, 83, 89, 91, 97, 102, 105, 111, 113 – plants and flowers © Arthur Balitskii/Shutterstock.com; cover and pp.8, 12, 21, 25, 34, 41, 46, 51, 58, 68, 69, 80, 87, 91, 102, 103, 113, 114, 123 – turtle © alyaBigJoy/Shutterstock.com; cover and pp.8, 18, 21, 28, 34, 42, 46, 55, 58, 66, 69, 77, 80, 91, 93, 102, 110, 113, 121, 128 – bee © alyaBigJoy/Shutterstock.com; cover and pp.8, 20, 21, 33, 34, 44, 46, 57, 58, 69, 80, 81, 91, 98, 102, 109, 113, 120 – birds © Arthur Balitskii/Shutterstock.com; cover and pp.8, 21, 31, 34, 45, 46, 58, 63, 69, 74, 80, 85, 91, 102, 107, 113, 122 – monkeys © Arthur Balitskii/Shutterstock.com; cover and pp.8, 21, 34, 46, 58, 69, 80, 91, 102, 113 – beetle © alyaBigJoy/Shutterstock.com; cover and pp.8, 21, 34, 46, 58, 69, 80, 91, 102, 113 – fish © Arthur Balitskii/Shutterstock.com; cover and pp.8, 21, 34, 46, 58, 69, 80, 91, 102, 113 – chameleon © Arthur Balitskii/Shutterstock.com; pp.4, 14, 19, 27, 37, 43, 53, 56, 64, 78, 86, 94, 100, 108, 116, 124 – frog © Arthur Balitskii/Shutterstock.com; pp.10, 23, 32, 50, 60, 71, 82, 99, 115 – ammonite fossil © Alejo Bernal/Shutterstock.com; pp.15, 26, 36, 48, 62, 75, 88, 104, 119 – snake © vinap/Shutterstock.com; pp.17, 30, 47, 65, 76, 92, 112 – starfish © alyaBigJoy/Shutterstock.com

Have you enjoyed this book? If so, find us on Facebook at **Summersdale Publishers**, on Twitter/X at **@Summersdale** and on Instagram and TikTok at **@summersdalebooks** and get in touch. We'd love to hear from you!

www.summersdale.com